RORSZAG   ROMA

BULGARIJA

ΕΛΛΑΣ

SHQIPERIJA

Yugoslavia — One Long Summer

COVER:
WOMAN FROM MACEDONIA
PHOTO D. KAŽIĆ

Yugoslavia –
One Long Summer

Text by Jara Ribnikar

McGRAW-HILL BOOK COMPANY
NEW YORK TORONTO LONDON

Yugoslavia — One long summer

With a little luck and a wisely chosen adviser, you can spend a long, bewitching summer in Yugoslavia.

It will be rich and generous, too, in its variegated impressions, in its rejuvenating peace (though you may be bone-tired at the end of any vigorous, colorful day), in the many friendships you will make. You will relive ancient days and savor the new. As you cross a mountain range, you may discover the surprises of an entirely new region — of colors and climes that change in an instant. There are other peoples and other customs; even the stone is a different color and the song of the peasants has a different ring to it.

Perhaps the gratest charm of this country lies in its diversity; perhaps it is in the different epochs living side by side. The land abounds in those fascinating traces of the past that we encounter wherever the strata of various cultures have been deposited one upon the other. This country still invites the extensive excavations of the archaeologist. It has already revealed enigmatic neolithic idols, strange jars from Butmir, and Illyrian situlae and Greek vases hiding underneath its fields and stones. On their surfaces they tell thrilling stories of battles and joy — as though they were the motion picture archives of a prehistoric time. Priceless golden masks of mighty warriors, shining helmets of Roman horsemen, mosaics rivaling Ravenna's, gay maenads, jewelry of the earliest Slavs — all these have been delivered from oblivion. The archeologists have stored up

V

countless treasures in the Yugoslav museums. But the promise of artefacts undiscovered still lures the scientist seeking the mysteries of antiquity.

Nations on the move and great tides of invaders have been unable to obliterate the artistry of our forebears preserved in stone on the surface of the earth. Scarred and maimed, the buildings, the sculpture, and the painting continue to live in our midst. We love ruins: they are a passion of twentieth-century man; patina and fragments work a spell upon us. You shall see how impressive the marble contours of the amphitheatre in Pula are in the sunlight, and what drama the span of its condensed time contains. There are medieval cathedrals, monasteries, and mansions that have been preserved intact in this land. The Orthodox monasteries and churches seem to stand at world's end. You will not even catch a glimpse of Milesheva or Sopochani until you stand before their gates. Hills and woods rise around Dechani like a heavy curtain.

There are masterpieces by anonymous painters, and the gouged eyes of their portraits are not always the work of vandalism or of time. Often it was superstition that devoured the eyes and the mouths of the beautiful paintings; for a piece of painted wall was needed as an antidote for sickness, a charm for love or happiness.

It is no wonder that vandalism and destruction touched this crossroad of the world, for these valleys have seen armies girded for plunder and conquest as long as Europe remembers itself. The first Slav states sprang into being defending themselves from the south, east, north, and the west.

This has been only the most cursory, superficial description of the wealth of art in this land, but perhaps it will lure you to your own journeys of discovery.

Let us return to the present. What makes Yugoslavia extraordinary today is not alone its cultural heritage but the amazing contrast of the modern and ancient forms of life existing side by side. To be sure, in recent years the sons of many peasants have become workers, artrists, generals, civil engineers — they have entered every calling. It is just as true that the intellectuals in the cities still nurture the cultural traditions of their people, although the towns are rapidly assuming that impersonal cosmopolitan trait wrought by industry and international commerce that assures the visitor he will feel at home in whatever Yugoslav city he visits. The town is indifferent to its environs. It is imbued with

VI

the ruthless impassiveness of asphalt. You will find this impassiveness reflected in the abstract art and introspective poetry of every major Yugoslav town in summer. And, of course, you will find the fine hotels, the helpful travel agents, the colorful taverns and nightclubs, the indispensable banks, and the fascinating museums that you search out in the cities of the world.

So it is in the towns that you will find the second half of the twentieth century. You will find it in the theatre programs and in the shop windows displaying ladies' shoes and all the latest fashions. Wait for Godot, see Pinter and Frisch, or be at Behanean loggerheads with the rest of the world. And of course there are the nightclubs — they are said to feature strip-tease numbers — but you need not go to nightclubs to find beautiful girls; they may be seen everywhere. Whatever type of feminine beauty appeals to you most, you will find represented here. Yugoslav women range from the natural blondes of Slovenia to the dark-complexioned beauties of Macedonia. The Montenegrin girls are proud, slim, and tall; the Bosnian, curvaceous and inscrutable; you may contemplate your ideal of pulchritude like an icon... and, behold, she speaks. Or you may consider the real icons, the Byzantine ones, more beautiful than the living ones. But that, to be sure, is all a matter of taste.

We need not guide you through the towns. You will be quite at home in them as you shop, or tour the museums, or visit the bank.

For the individual, incomparable view of Yugoslavia, turn away from the main road or express railway. You will find yourself in a strange mood. The shepherd tending his flock plays his pipe. His notes will disturb your formless reverie. What is it that he knows? He is as young or as old as the hills, in garments long since bleached by the sun. How is it that his call speaks so eloquentl yto you?

Perhaps you will come upon a big village wedding, with dancing and eating and drinking, with music and song, lasting several days and nights. The brisk *kolo* dance of Shumadiya is a merry maze of faultlessly tripping feet. You will discover that the Serbian peasant is an intriguing personalty — a born optimist — and he is familiar with politics, too. You shall also meet the *guslar* playing on his single-stringed instrument. Crowds listen to his improvised songs for hours on end; his words are a fathomless store of unwritten wisdom. Many *guslas* are works of art, adorned with fantastic ornamentation on the wood.

The men and women in these remote regions wear the authentic national costume of ancient origin, unlike anything you will see elsewhere in Europe. In Macedonia the hair style is made to suit the costume. In the low cabins of the towering Bosnian mountains (which you can reach only if you hire a surefooted little mountain pony) live the taciturn people whom prosperity and the blandishments of civilization have not lured down into the valley. It seems that decades would be needed before these people could adapt to the world of the railway and road, of the telephone and television. But working at his distinctive paintings, in the art academy of Belgrade, is the red-bearded young artist Falil, who was born in a cabin of this sort. What prompted him to go to the city? Who advised him to do so? Perhaps we are not so far removed from the mountaineers after all.

The dances of the mountaineers reflect their temperament — they have no instrumental accompaniment; there is only the music of the human voice or the rhythm of the steps. One of their picturesque dances is the *Glamoch Kolo*.

In Kosovo and Metokhiya are most of the medieval monasteries, where there are world-famous murals. Here the Shkupetars are mingled with the Serbs and Montenegrins. You can see there the typical Shkupetar turrets; behind their walls live families for whom the patriarchal rules are more tightly binding than any law of state.

But you cannot spend the summer along the byways, in the bright sun and enveloping dust. The roads that take you to the most interesting parts of Serbia are not always the best, and you should travel them fast and forget them. A stroll through the Serbian Middle Ages will enchant everyone who is drawn to Yugoslavia by its folklore. Choose any place: Grachanitsa, Pech, Dechani, or Studenitsa, Sopochani, Milesheva. Go to Macedonia, and on your way you will see strange customs and authentic folk art. As you return from Milesheva, you will suddenly find yourself in the Wild West — the endless Peshter Plateau, sparsely inhabited, with vast flocks tended by a shepherd wrapped in cloth of his own making. The region is famed far and wide for its cheese. The air is crisp. We are over three thousand feet high. The sky is an infinite sweep that begins only an arm's length away.

But what will enchant you most in your journey through the Orthodox Middle Ages is Ohrid. So, if you are pressed by time, go straight to Ohrid.

VIII

There you will view a sea in miniature, excellent fish, trout, several of the most beautiful monasteries, the most precious icons, and frescoes, too. The lay architecture has provided inspiration to Le Corbusier. You will see fishing in ancient boats, outstretched nets, and girls bleaching linen, just as it was promised in the ancient song. There will be pleasant swimming in fresh water without the need to become accustomed to salt water.

From Ohrid you can go to Lake Prespa. Visit the village of Kurbinovo; go to the hillock where stands a solitary church consecrated to St George and you will see the lake that marks the joining of the frontiers of Greece, Yugoslavia, and Albania. In Macedonia you ought also to visit Lake Doyran and see the peculiar method of fishing with specially trained cormorants.

Next year you may wish to see other Yugoslav lakes. Lake Skadar in Montenegro will remind you of the creation of the world: the fingers, the head, and the shoulders of the earth seem to be slowly growing out of the water, overcoming the bogs, the mud, and the darkness. It would be unfair not to tell you of the emerald waters overflowing in thundering waterfalls from lake to lake at Plitvitse. And what about Slovenia? The phantom silver lakes of Mount Triglav hover amid the peaks of the Alps, and dramatic Lake Bohin and Alpine green ornament the other side. Then comes the world-renowned Lake Bled. This is the lake that heals the nerves. Its therapeutic promise has made it famous. In these times its tranquil peace is sundered by the jazz entertainment that rends the evening air as accompaniment to boisterous dances. But these are contemporary diversions that need not interfere with those travelers who have come for Lake Bled's rejuvenating calm. Solitude and peace are always there for those who seek them; the woods that surround Lake Bled stretch for miles.

You may easily find a quiet, pleasant spot for your family if you have decided on a rest in the woods; there are still vast tracts of woodland in Slovenia, Croatia, Serbia, Montenegro, and Macedonia. Bosnia is the richest. It possesses the last remaining primeval forest in Europe. There you may come face to face with bear, wild goat, wild boar, the eagle, the vulture, the fox, and other wild creatures... And with packs of wolves. Hunters come from far away for the game here. You may even have the good fortune to glimpse the legendary white wolf roaming alone over the canyon of the river Drina.

IX

Perhaps you are growing impatient and asking yourself: But where is the sea? Yugoslavia is famous as the Adriatic Riviera. Before I took you to Yugoslavia's incomparable seashores, I wanted you to discover that my country is not merely the Adriatic. I should also have told you about the endless plain of Voivodina, with the undulating grain, ancient windmills, and thoroughbred studs; about the flint-hard stone of Montenegro and its poetry; about the vineyards, gardens, flowers. But let all this be. We shall go to the Adriatic, though it is a sight that defies description and truly must be seen to be believed.

If you have never seen it before, you will be astonished at the azure of the Adriatic. It glows with a blue all its own. Its amazing hue may come from the purplish-green algae living in it and from the composition of its bottom of stone. Or perhaps it owes its beauty to all the things that have foundered in it while the Yugoslav coast has been sinking through the centuries. If you are curious to see sunken towns, you can find them easily. More than a thousand islands follow the indented coastline; there are shallow coves and deep fjords, white beaches, caves invaded by the sea, steep cliffs and then gentle coves again, and harbors for big ships and countless fishing ports in miniature. This intriguing panorama unfolds all the way down from Kopar in the north to southernmost Ultsin.

In ancient times the Illyrians, the Greeks, the Romans, the Goths, and the Avars waged war to possess the Adriatic; the Slavs finally won it in the sevneht century and fought for their consolidation between two mighty powers — the expanding Franks in the West, and the powerful Byzantines in the East. If you are one of the growing number of tourists who wish to learn of the distant past as you relax in the present, you will find something here of Rome, of Greece, of Byzantium, and of Illyria.

You may also pay a visit to Dubrovnik. That white coffer of stone, full of gems, lying like a small heaven on earth on the deep blue sea of the southern Adriatic, is worth it, I assure you. No tourist advertisements and colorful folders have been able to render it commonplace. Indeed it has all the variety the sophisticate may crave. There is room for the dreamer in Dubrovnik, too... and for the art historian, the art lover, and the artist. The athlete, the writer, the student, the weary and the bored — each can find a place for himself there, a sanctuary of his own or the sweep of space. Dubrovnik has much to give.

And so, it should not surprise you. We start our photographs with the sea after all. Let it be Dubrovnik to begin with.

X

The sea. The coves and cathedrals. A thousand Islands

Since the beginning of the seventh century, when it was founded, *Pages 4-5, 7, 8, 9, 10, 11, 13, 14, 15, 16*
Dubrovnik has been built up and expanded, demolished, built up
anew, on the old core of stone, growing prettier and extending beyond
the bastions which concealed its wealth from many enemies. It has
survived for centuries by sheer diplomatic skill, cunning, and talent
evading the dangers placed in its way by history. From the traces of
old Christian architecture to the masterpieces of stately Romanesque
(the Cathedral, the Church of St Blasius, the monasteries of the *Page 12*
Minorites and Dominicans), and down to the simple works of the
early Gothic (the church of the Minorites) with several works in the
transitional Romanesque-Gothic (monasteries), and then by instilling
elements of the Renaissance into the half-demolished Gothic buildings,
Dubrovnik evolved a Gothic-Romanesque synthesis that lent the old
city its principal charm. These are the Rector's Palace, the Divona
Palace (the customs house), the city clock tower, the palaces and
summer mansions. The church of the Holy Savior and several pa-
trician palaces in pure Renaissance style were built during the latter
part of the sixteenth century; and in the seventeenth, the baroque
reached Dubrovnik. The city walls (up to 5.30 metres in thickness) *Page 6*
girding the historic part of the city are still a unique fortification. In

1667 a severe earthquake damaged part of the city. Dubrovnik soon revived, developing with feverish haste according to the plans of local and foreign city planners; the historical contours of the Romanesque, Gothic, and Renaissance blended with its new features, which, like a solid architectural museum, attract all those who gaze with longing from the sun-bathed beaches far into the past.

Split is a city whose everlasting breath of antiquity combines with the rhythm of the present day. The old city was born inside the walls *Page 20* of the palace that Diocletian, an Illyrian shepherd and emperor of Rome, ordered to be built when he retired from the affairs of state.

The palace, built on the seashore, for centuries offered haven and protection to the population, withstanding onslaughts during the migration of nations and the whims of Nature. The palace architecture is a story of past epochs.

The Peristyle was turned into the vestibule of a Christian temple; *Page 19* the small antique temple into a baptistery; the bas-relief inside is an *Page 21* image of the first king of Croatia as a token of early Slav statehood. The emperor's stately mausoleum was turned into a cathedral in the eighth century, to which access is given by a pair of doors richly *Pages 17, 18* carved by Andriya Buvina. Today, Split looks out upon the sea and world outside the walls, though it is closely linked with the ancient palace. The port is as busy as a beehive, the Riviera swarms with bathers. The Maryan Park offers an infinite vista of sea and islands. A short distance from Split lies Trogir. The cathedral square is one of the most beautiful sights. It is enhanced by a magnificent loggia and by the mighty cathedral, whose unforgettable portal was wrought in the thirteenth century by the master artist, Radovan.

Page 22 Zadar is a town of dark-green parks and antique pillars round which the colorful people gather at the sumptuous fruit, vegetable, and flower market. On the Roman forum rises the famous old church of St Donat, which was built in the ninth century.

Pages 24, 25 The antique buildings in Pula are famous: the impressive amphitheater built by Augustus is a spacious, arcaded three-story building,

XII

the scene once of fighting gladiators, and of film festivals today; the Porta Aurea has cannelured pilasters and Corinthian capitals; the temple of Augustus and Roma is in the severely logical arrangement of the Roman style of construction. In the acrid landscape of Istria, the basilica of Porech is an especially attractive goal of the traveler. Its oldest mosaics go back to the fourth century, the famous ones that remind one of Ravenna having been wrought by order of Bishop Euphrasius in the sixth century. At the lower end of the long central nave, the mosaics shimmer upon the walls of the apse in their festive and severe magnificence.

Color plate between pages 22 and 23

The Adriatic coast has more than a thousand islands, large and small, the world of fishermen, winegrowers, stone-cutters and of beautiful lace.

Susak, the farthest in the upper Adriatic and also the most retiring, has preserved many ancient elements and developed many distinctive features. It is unusual for its dialect, national costume, and customs. Its sandy soil is suitable for grape growing, the only crop on the island. The Susak women's festive costume, a stiff starched, short, wide skirt, resembles the costumes worn in the mountains of Greece.

Page 26

Rab is a wooded island. Its old cathedral offers pleasant architectural reminiscences. Pag is an island of grazing sheep, and of fine lace. Hvar has the oldest theatre in the country, churches and palaces with Gothic and Renaissance facades along shady streets.

Pages 30, 31, 34

It is easy to get to the island of Korchula from Orebich, the old seamen's town on the Pelyeshats Peninsula. The town of Korchula, a Dubrovnik in miniature, stands in the midst of wooded hills. The ancient city walls, the bulky defense turrets, the beautiful cathedral lend the small town a most striking silhouette. Mlyet is an island of special natural beauty, with a picturesque lake set down in the heart of green forests. The twelfth-century Benedictine monastery lends this enchanting spot a distinctive architectural air.

Pages 32, 33

From Dubrovnik southeastward many travelers proceed by way of Mlini and Hertsegnovi to the Bay of Tivat. Numerous localities

XIII

stud the Gulf of Kotor over which majestically rises Mount Lovchen.

Page 39 Two tiny islands, St Yuray and Our Lady of Shkerpyel, seem to float calmly and lightly on the water's surface. From the town of Kotor, with the twelfth-century cathedral of St Tripun, a road runs to Budva, Milocher, and Sveti Stefan. Once the summer haunt of painters who went in for fishing as a hobby, Sveti Stefan is now, after conservation by architects, an ancient and at the same time a highly comfortable place, inviting to the most sophisticated tourist.

The Yugoslav Alps. Noble peaks. Naked crags and the endless Pannonian lowland

Several mountain ranges intertwine in Yugoslavia. They have produced dramatic and tame landscapes in which the mountain climber, Alpinist, and the everyday Excursionist can find what they seek: tranquility, endless vistas, game, rest, and thrills. The highest *Page 40* peak in Yugoslavia is Mount Triglav in the Julian Alps in Slovenia, 2,863 metres. Then comes Mount Korab in Macedonia, 2,764 metres; and Tito's Peak on Mount Shara in Macedonia, 2,747 metres.

The highest peak in Montenegro is Bobotov Kuk on Mount Durmitor, 2,528 metres, which is a thrilling wild mountain untouched by the mountain climber's mapping. The best-known Bosnian mountains are clothed with dense conifers of many centuries, spotted with mountain huts and lodges. They are Byelashnitsa, Romaniya, Yahorina, and Pren (between 1,396 and 1,012 metres). Mountains attractive for their rich vegetation and meadow flowers, coniferous woods, and game preserves are the pleasant, tame Serbian mountains, *Pages 46, 47* about a thousand metres high, like Zlatibor, Tara, Stolovi and Goliya. Kopaonik is 2,017 metres. Probably the most attractive *Page 43* mountains for the Alpinist are the Julian and Kamnik Alps (Triglav and Grintovets). The many mountain chalets, the bivouacs, and shel-

XIV

ters are evidence here of the mountain-climbing and tourist traditions. Modern roads plunge into the glacial valleys beneath the climber's delight of the steep cliffs. The seven lakes of Triglav lie along the popular route through the Triglav valley. Here the mountain climber and Alpinist will find various types of gentians, Alpine roses, rhododendrons, and Edelweiss.

Pages 41, 45

Glacial lakes. Cascades and waterfalls. Warm lakes of Macedonia. The wonder of the canyons

Some people like to sit by a river, others prefer to explore lakes; some prefer the wild and the placid fresh waters to the ceaseless lapping waves of the salt sea water.

There are fifteen large lakes in Yugoslavia, the largest of which are Lakes Skadar, Ohrid, Prespa and Doyran. They possess the breadth of the sea, and the intimacy of natural enclosures.

The sixteen Plitvitsa lakes lie amid the peaks of Mala Kapela and Plyeshivitsa. One below the other, they are linked by foaming waterfalls and cascades of unreal, translucent hues; from light blue to ultramarine, from green to the most varied greenish-blue mists and crystal-white froths. Many stories and tales have been spun around Plitvitse, both happy and sad, both nuptual and suicidal.

Page 54

Bled and Bohin are two famous lakes in Slovenia. Lake Bled is warm. It resembles a gigantic palm containing just enough water that men may not lose themselves in it, and swimmers or boatsmen feel at home in it from the very first day. Lake Bohin is another matter. It is a genuine glacial lake, second in beauty only to some of the Swiss. lakes. The silver cliffs, the dark-green woods, the fresh restless surface through which flows the sumptuous Sava lend this detached spot an atmosphere of poetry and mystery.

Page 44

In the Serbian mountains are some lakes known and dear only to the mountain climber, the most beautiful of which lies on Mount Kopaonik. Bosnia and Macedonia also have numerous dark, unknown mountain lakes hedged in on all sides by woods.

XV

You shall often encounter the angler on the shores of the lakes and on the banks of the mountain streams, for the green and blue waters in the canyons and woods are a treasure trove. The canyons of the Tara, Piva, Drina (river courses over a thousand metres deep), Neretva and Moracha, Vrbas or the Bohinska Bistritsa, Krka and Una, Tsetina or Radika, Socha — all these rivers and many lakes are the habitat of trout and salmon.

Pages 50, 51
Page 52

Serbian and Macedonian medieval art

On the shores of Lake Ohrid stand monasteries and churches. In the tenth century, Ohrid was a center of Slav culture. Near the Albanian frontier stands St Naum's, a small church consecrated to the Archangel Michael. It is there that Kliment and Naum did their work. They were disciples of Cyril and Methodius, who spread the Gospel in the Slav literary tongue. The most important monastery church on the shore of Lake Ohrid is St Sofia's. It was built by Archbishop Leon during the first half of the eleventh century. It is the most precious monument of fresco painting from that period on South Slav soil. St Jovan of Kaneo's, a small church on a cliff over-looking the lake, is like a large flower. St Kliment's, which was built in 1295 by Progon Zgur, son-in-law of the Byzantine emperor, Andro-nicus II, contains frescoes interesting also because we are familiar with the names of the painters, Mihailo and Eutihije which is some-thing very exceptional. From this church come the most beautiful and the oldest icons in Macedonia, including the late thirteenth or early fourteenth-century icon of the Crucifixion. The foremost icon workshops were at Ohrid, Dechani, Pech, and Moracha.

The famous church of St Panteleimon is also in Macedonia, at Nerezi. It was built by Alexius I Comnenus in 1164. The frescoes of extraordinary beauty lay beneath a coat of paint until 1926. By their plastic forms, which no longer contain the stiffness of fresco painting familiar until then, by the uninhibited presentation of the human

Page 59

Page 70
Page 58

Page 71

Pages 60, 61

XVI

being, the frescoes at Nerezi attain the peak in Byzantine painting on Slav soil and constitute a change in its development.

The church of the Virgin Mary at Studenitsa was built by the great Serbian zhupan, Stevan Nemanya, toward the end of the twelfth and at the beginning of the thirteenth century. The stately frescoes for the first time betoken the Serbian idiosyncrasies. The Studenitsa Monastery lies in a thick wood in the mountains. There are three churches within the monastery walls, the most important of which has been consecrated to the Virgin Mary. *Pages 68, 69*

The monastery church of Milesheva was built by the Serbian king, Vladislav, c. 1230. With their vivid portraits of the founders, the fresco painters Dimitriye, Teodor, and Georgiye indicated that they had freed themselves from Byzantine influence. *Pages 62, 63*

The Patriarchate of Pech, which was built during the first half of the thirteenth century, raises its domes at a point where the Rugovo Gorge opens out into a lowland. The church of the Holy Apostle, the oldest of the churches of the Patriarchate of Pech, was built by Arseniye, successor to St Sava. Its frescoes reveal postures that resemble antiquity in a severe and solemn style. *Page 64*

Color plate between pages 64 and 65

The Sopochani Monastery is the climax. Unadorned on the outside, the monastery church, which was built by the King Stefan Urosh in 1256, was adorned ten years later with frescoes so perfect that this monument may be termed the Sistine Chapel of the Serbian Middle Ages. The feeling for clearness and joy of life and antique harmony combine here with oriental spirituality. *Pages 66, 67*

The church of Our Lady of Lyevich at Prizren was built by the King Milutin in 1307 on the foundations of an old basilica. The walls, which had been whitewashed, were cleaned in 1953. The colors shone forth again, the figures and countenances, animals and plants that were uncovered were imbued, but for a certain archaic air, with the fresh feeling of life.

The Grachanitsa Monastery is perhaps the most beautiful of the forty-odd churches built by the King Milutin. The king-founder and his famous queen, Simonida, daughter of the emperor Andronicus Paleologus, are portrayed on the frescoes. The stately architecture is a harmonious expression of the Serbo-Byzantine style.

The greatest church of the Serbian Middle Ages, the Dechani Monastery, was built by Stefan Urosh III Dechanski, and his son, later the Emperor Dushan, between the years 1327 and 1357. More than a thousand paintings tell a heavenly and worldly story in detached compositions and in cycles.

The church of St Andreyash was built near Skoplje in 1389, at the time of the Battle of Kosovo Plain, The founder was Andriya, brother of Marko Kraljević, the legendary prince. This small church beside the hydroelectric power plant on the river Treska deserves tobeseen.

The building of foundation churches and monasteries was a custom of long standing. Falling back before the Ottoman tide, the princes of northern Serbia built the churches and monasteries of the "Morava School": Ravanitsa, Lyubostinya, Manasiya, and Kalenich.

The Kalenich Monastery was built by the Cup-bearer, Bogdan his wife Militsa, and brother Petar between 1407 and 1413. It is held that the frescoes in the Kalenich Monastery are the last great accomplishment in medieval Serbian art. The tender drawing, the gentle colorwork, and harmonious composition conjure up the rather sad vision of the bygone way of life of the Middle Ages.

The country and the people. Historical reminiscences

The Yugoslav national territory comprises a varied ethnic community with an exceptionally rich cultural past, which is due to the geopolitical position of the Balkan Peninsula, as a link between the East and the West, and to the central position held by the Yugoslav ethnic group in it. Ownig to this, the Balkan Peninsula has always been an objective of war, of strategic designs, ethnic currents, and migrations. The cultural and ethnic outline reveals the presence of several powerful factors that were responsible for the making of the cultural and historical features of the entire area. Here cultural currents, ethnic and political influences alternated in a number of strata. The Illyrians, Thracians, Scythians, Hellenes, Romans, Byzantines, Florentines, Magyars, Turks, Austrians — these were

XVIII

merely the most outstanding of the molders of the history and culture of the Balkan area. The Slav tribes advanced into this ethnic and culturally rich area during the sixth century. They completed settling it in the seventh, when they had taken a firm hold on the outermost points of what have for over twelve hundred years constituted the boundaries of the Yugoslav peoples.

In their new homeland the Yugoslav tribes were exposed to the unceasing political, military, and cultural pressure or powers fighting for hegemony in the Balkans; the history of the ethnic, political and cultural survival of the South Slav tribes is a history of pressures and influences and of their being overcome. It was during the centuries of struggle with these influences that the national individuality of the Yugoslav peoples took shape and developed.

Farming and warring were two indivisible components in the historical features of the past of the Yugoslav. A peasant tied to his plot of hard and primitively worked land, a gifted stone-cutter, sculptor, and fresco-painter with an urge to embellish and to enrich his hard existence by means of his own beautiful, harmonious handi-work, the Yugoslav became a warrior at a moment's notice whenever anyone attempted to endanger his peaceful labors from abroad.

Upon the sources of this vigor sprang up and developed the first Slav states: in the seventh century, a Slovene state under Prince Samo; in the middle of the eighth century, Rashka under Prince Visheslav, and a Croatian state under Prince Trpimir; Zeta under prince Vladimir in the tenth century, Bosnia under Ban Kulin in the twelfth. The mightiest South Slav state in the tenth century was the Macedonian state under Emperor Samuilo. Under the King Tomislav, Croatia reached the peak of its medieval political power, becoming a kingdom c. 925. Rashka under the house of Nemanyich developed between the twelfth and the fourteenth century into the mightiest state in the Balkans; Dushan, son of Stevan Dechanski, was crowned emperor in 1346. Dushan's Codex from that period is the most important Yugoslav cultural-historic and legal document of the Middle Ages. Bosnia attained the peak of its power under the King Tvrtko, who brought parts of Serbia, Croatia, Dalmatia, and the Littoral under his power towards the end of the fourteenth century. During the latter half of the fourteenth century, the Turks moved inexorably into the Balkans. Defeated at the river Maritsa and on Kosovo Plain, Serbia became a vassal state and lost sovereignty in 1459. Soon after, in 1463, Bosnia fell. Montenegro lost sovereignty in 1499, but the Montenegrin tribes resisted until the end of the seventeenth century, when sovereignty was revived under Bishop Danilo Petrovich. The greatest Yugoslav epic poet, Petar Petrovich Nyegosh, was a member of this family. The Yugoslav peoples had a historical part to play in the Balkan Peninsula also during the period of Turkish expansion towards Central Europe: the Yugoslav peoples were a decisive military factor in the unceasing, exhausting work of wearing down the Turkish military power. Perpetually doing sentry duty along the boundaries of the marches, dispersed as military crews in the fortresses and citadels along the route of the Ottoman advance into Central Europe, or waging unorganized, mobile wars (the haiduks and the uskoks) with the Turks, the Yugoslav peoples made one of the most important contributions to the defense of all Europe against the invasion at the height of the Ottoman empire.

Serbia freed itself from the Turkish yoke during the First and the Second Insurrection, under Karadjordje in 1804 and under Milosh Obrenovich in 1815. The nineteenth century was noted for the intensification of ideas of unification in the Yugoslav territories. Unable to bring it about politically, this aspiration found powerful expression in culture. The foremost Yugoslav minds — Kopitar in Slovenia, Lyudevit Gay and Strossmayer in Croatia, Vuk Karadzhich and Dyura Danichich in Serbia, and others, developing the literary tongue in their several territories, nurtured strong cultural ties among their nations. At the beginning of the twentieth century, Yugoslav unification assumed definite political form in the demand for the liberation of the Yugoslav territories from Turkish and Austro-Hungarian domination. The Great War having ended, the first Yugoslav state was founded under the House of Karadjordjevich. But the several Yugoslav nations became equals only in the Liberation War of 1941 to 1945, when a federal socialist community was founded.

ILLUSTRATIONS

SCSM
VRV

33

45

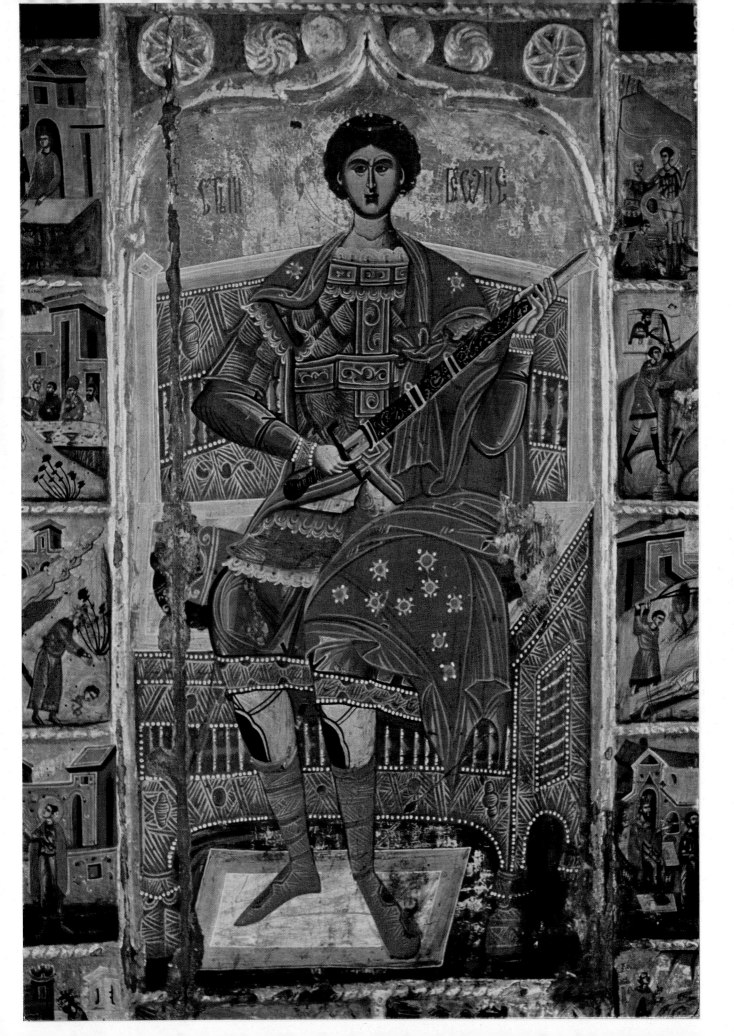

71

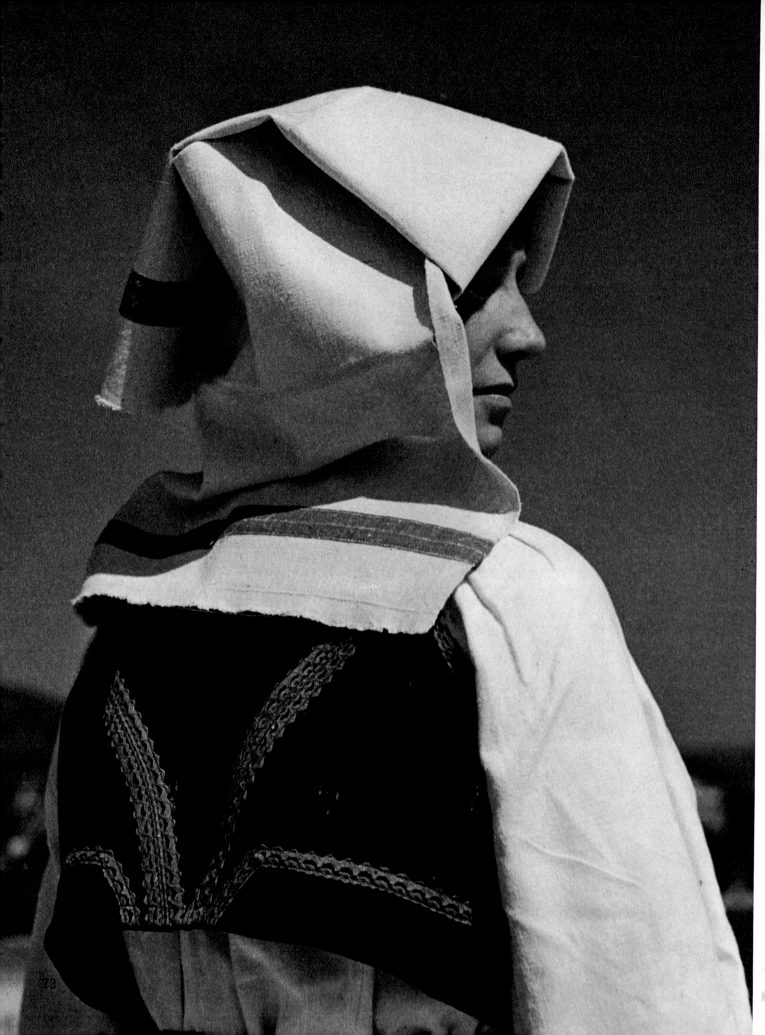

93